Nature Truths

Using Creation to Reveal Biblical Truths About God and the Way the World Works

A 12-Week Devotional Study

SHERRI SELIGSON

© 2022 Sherri Seligson. All rights reserved.
Scripture quotations are from the ESV® Bible (The Holy Bible, English Standard Version®),
©2001 Crossway Bibles, a publishing ministry of Good News Publishers.
Used by permission. All rights reserved.

Download Your FREE Activity Guide Resource to Accompany This Book
Visit: www.ckonlinestore.com and add the Activity Guide to your cart.
Checkout using code: TRUTHINNATURE

One of my favorite things about God's Word is that it's living and active (Hebrews 4:12). We can read a verse we think we know and see much we haven't seen before. Or, verses that haven't made much sense in the past suddenly do. This is exactly what happened when I read Sherri's devotionals.

Sherri's explanations of the nature truths embedded in Scriptures brought Truth to light. I never fully understood the power in some verses because I didn't know enough about nature to appreciate the illustrations God used to His points. Thanks to Sherri's understandings and compelling writing, I learned important things about God and me. I'm grateful! I'm hoping Sherri will immediately work on another devotional. I'm ready for more!

I've known Sherri for several years. She loves the Lord, is consistently joyful, excellent at what she does, and passionate about learning, parents, and children. And, as you'll see when you read this, she understands nature. That's an understatement!

Get ready to be challenged, inspired, and surprised. Whether you're already very nature smart or willing to grow in your understanding, there's something for you here.

Kathy Koch, PhD
Founder, Celebrate Kids
Associate Founder, Ignite the Family

Like a walk in the woods, from the moment you see and feel Sherri Seligson's 12-week devotional, you get the idea that you're going to experience something refreshingly meaningful. As you open the book it's as though you're on a guided nature walk... through the Word of God. If you enjoy nature, journaling, and reflection, you're going to love *Nature Truths*.

Todd Wilson
Founder of The Familyman and
The Smiling Homeschooler

Nature Truths is an easy-to-read devotional that beautifully weaves scripture and nature to draw the reader into a closer relationship with the One who created all that is. Whether this book is used in a group setting or one-on-one, all will marvel at the wonder of God.

Connie Albers
Author of Parenting Beyond the Rules
Owner of the Equipped to Be Podcast

Through *Nature Truths*, Sherri leads us towards a more full sacramental view of nature - the mingling of heaven and earth and our place in this dance. She demonstrates that science leads us towards our Creator. I enjoyed this study and will pass on this book to my three teenage daughters.

Sarah Stonestreet
Co-Host of the Strong Women Podcast
Colson Center Fellow Cohort Director

Table of Contents

Week 1: God Is The Creator of All and Upholds All — *The Hydrologic Cycle* — Page 13

Week 2: We Are Uniquely Created — *Sunsets* — Page 23

Week 3: Our Identity — *Grafting* — Page 33

Week 4: The Fear of the Lord is Wisdom — *Earth's Atmosphere* — Page 43

Week 5: The Lord's Forgiveness — *Infinity* — Page 53

Week 6: The Nourishment of God's Word — *Taste* — Page 63

Week 7: God's Timeline for Us — *Dormancy* — Page 73

Week 8: God Understands Our Hurts — *Chemical Reactions* — Page 83

Week 9: Our Words Are Powerful — *Salt* — Page 93

Week 10: Joy Versus Happiness — *Laughter* — Page 103

Week 11: Selflessness — *The Dead Sea* — Page 113

Week 12: Restlessness — *Migration* — Page 123

**Download your Nature Truths Activity Guide PDF at:

A Note From the Author

Have you ever wondered why so many people feel closer to God when they are outside in nature? There is something quieting and peaceful about walking along a forest path in the fall. We marvel when we stand at the ocean shore, watching the waves rhythmically move in. A clear, night sky beckons us to pause whatever we're doing and look up.

I had been pondering those thoughts one day while I was cleaning my windows. Suddenly, I noticed something that made me stop in my tracks. In an instant, my demeanor went from "daily-grungy-chores-blah" to "heart-lifting-cheery-smile." What caused it?

Tiny fingerprints.

You see, just a few weeks earlier (no judging as to how long it took me to clean!) my daughter-in-law and one-year-old granddaughter had come for a visit. These toddler fingerprints were an instant reminder of that.

But there was more to it. I wondered how an "organized smudge" could evoke such an emotional response from me. Well, it has to do with those fingerprints belonging to someone specific - someone to whom my heart is attached. And when I see them, her sweet face comes right to mind. I think of her reaching up to me. I remember her little hugs.

There is another One whose fingerprints cause me to stop in my tracks, changing my countenance almost immediately. I see these prints on things in creation. *You see, when God makes something, His fingerprints are all over it.* What He crafts is covered by His unique "organized smudges."

So when I step outside to get the mail and suddenly see a lovely rainbow stretching across the sky, I pause to marvel at how light behaves for our good. As I observe the awesome complexity in creation when I study organisms through a microscope, I am taken aback that my God spoke them into being. When I see a hummingbird dip its perfectly-shaped beak into a flower in order to drink in its sweet nectar, I am overcome by the detailed connection between the flower's unique features that lure the bird to disperse its pollen to other flowers - something the flower cannot do on its own.

His fingerprints are everywhere.

In this nature-truth study, you will read a passage of the Bible and then spend a few days diving into the truths behind it. The wonder of creation will unfold as an understanding of nature helps to uncover the handprints of our Creator-God, giving us greater insight into His Word.

We should never be afraid to explore the world around us. It truly exists to give testimony and glory to the One who made it! Psalm 19:1-2 *"The heavens declare the glory of God, and the sky above proclaims His handiwork. Day to day pours out speech, and night to night reveals knowledge."*

My prayer is that by exploring God's Word through the lens of nature-truths, it will open your hearts to His power, majesty, and loving kindness and cause you, along with His creation, to give Him glory!

Look for God's fingerprints today!

How to use This Book

The Bible is God's living Word that touches our souls. It is timeless; transcending centuries and cultures, yet is still relevant to the human heart today. Even with a lifetime of study, each passage can be new and fresh to meet us where we are. Keep that in mind when using this book. This study is for *you*, so use it in a way that works best for you.

On the surface, this book is outlined in a way that will cover 12 weeks of deep, reflective Bible study to fill you with wonder. Each week addresses a truth from Scripture that is expanded when we explore what man has learned by studying God's creation. The Bible passage includes a highlighted segment in order to dive into the Nature Truth of the week.

Next, the passage is followed by two explanatory sections:

> **What is the text saying?** covers the background - the circumstances of the passage's writing, who the audience was, or a bit about the overall Bible book the passage is from.
>
> **What is the nature-truth behind the verses?** focuses on the highlighted Nature Truth verse which will expand the meaning, based on God's revelation in His creation.

Officially, Day 1 would consist of reading the passage, reading the two sections that follow, and then completing the Day 1 material. Then each day afterward, you would just complete the respective day's study. That way you would complete a lesson in a week.

However, we have given you large spaces for writing, drawing and reflection. Because there is a nature component to this study, you might want to read through the text and the two following sections and then take some time to sit on your porch and sketch something you see outside, particularly something that has to do with the current lesson. The first week, for example, talks about the hydrologic cycle. So go outside, look at the clouds and write or make a sketch about what you see. Think of the difference between white, fluffy clouds and looming, dark storm clouds. Spend time in prayer as you reflect on how although we have no control of the weather, God upholds us and is in control. That could be a day of study in itself.

I also find Bible memorization and journaling extremely helpful to the study of Scripture. So here is a course of study that incorporates the above components into a two-week-per-segment format:

Day 1 - Ask God to reveal His truths to you. Read the Bible passage and the two explanatory sections.
Day 2 - Journal some initial thoughts about what you read on Day 1.
Day 3 - Do Day 1 lesson.
Day 4 - Write the highlighted passage and begin memorizing it.
Day 5 - Do Day 2 lesson.
Day 6 - Reread the Bible passage, sketch, journal.

Day 7 - Do Day 3 lesson.

Day 8 - Do Day 4 lesson.

Day 9 - Meditate on the things you have been learning and journal about them.

Day 10 - Do Day 5 lesson.

I encourage you not to get caught up in the numbered days. They are just there to help you navigate through this study, particularly if you are doing it with others.

Take this time to savor God's Word. Pray before you begin each day and ask God to reveal Himself to you. Savor the sweet wonder that comes from seeing God's mighty fingerprints in creation and what He has for you from His Word each day!

Week 1:
God is the Creator of All and Upholds All - The Hydrologic Cycle
Read Job 36:24-33

Job 36:24-33

²⁴ *Remember to extol His work, of which men have sung.*

²⁵ *All mankind has looked on it; man beholds it from afar.*

²⁶ *Behold, God is great, and we know Him not; the number of His years is unsearchable.*

²⁷ **For He draws up the drops of water; they distill his mist in rain,**

²⁸ **which the skies pour down and drop on mankind abundantly.**

²⁹ *Can anyone understand the spreading of the clouds, the thunderings of His pavilion?*

³⁰ *Behold, He scatters His lightning about Him and covers the roots of the sea.*

³¹ *For by these He judges peoples; He gives food in abundance.*

³² *He covers His hands with the lightning and commands it to strike the mark.*

³³ *Its crashing declares His presence; the cattle also declare that He rises.*

1) What is the text saying? The book of Job is an interesting account where two stories are happening at the same time. God is having dealings with Satan who has accused Job of honoring God only because he has experienced health and wealth. Simultaneously, Job experiences great losses, and he and his friends try to understand the reason behind the suffering. Job finally rests in trusting God's goodness and in the hope of his deliverance. Thus, the book is an account to encourage us that even if there are no clear explanations to disasters or challenges we might go through, we can trust God and praise Him.

This lesson's Bible passage is a portion of Elihu's comments to Job. Elihu is Job's friend, and in verses 24-33, he is describing God's great work of creation, highlighting how God does nothing in a small way. If we understand that the mighty visible works in our world display God's wisdom, power, and goodness, then we can trust His care for us. We cannot see the full picture, and we must recognize that God is omnipotent (all powerful), and He is in control. In fact, we know that every person, even one who has not heard the good news of Jesus Christ, has the benefit of seeing how God reveals Himself through His creation (Romans 1:19-20) - something we can marvel with our eyes. Because God is in control of everything, indeed He is greatly to be praised.

2) What is the nature-truth behind the verses? Our highlighted verses reveal something absolutely amazing. You see, the book of Job is believed to be written over 3,000 years ago. Yet, the writer shares some interesting scientific facts about the hydrologic cycle of Earth. If you don't know what the hydrologic cycle is, the name should give you a clue. The prefix "hydro" means water, and a cycle refers to a series of events that are regularly repeated in the same order. And, indeed, that is what a hydrologic cycle is. It is the continuous process by which water is circulated throughout the Earth and its atmosphere.

Beginning in our oceans, lakes, and rivers, liquid water is heated by the sun, causing some of its individual molecules to gain enough energy to become gaseous water. We call that water vapor. You can see water vapor when you are heating a pot of water on the stove and finally see that steam rise out of the pot, letting you know it's time to put the pasta in. This vaporization of water is called evaporation.

Well, once water evaporates it rises in the air because it's lighter than the air molecules around it. As it rises it cools, because with higher altitudes temperatures are cooler. When water vapor cools, it eventually becomes liquid water again. And it must do this on a hard surface. It finds tiny dust particles in the air and condenses on them. This is the process of condensation. And that is what forms clouds. In fact, you could say that clouds are just tiny bits of dusty-water droplets. That's not very poetic, but it is scientifically true.

As these condensed droplets collect, the droplets of water become heavier until they are too heavy to remain in the air any longer. They begin to fall back to Earth in the form of rain, snow, or other moisture. This process is called precipitation. So, water travels from the Earth to the sky and back to Earth again: evaporation, condensation, precipitation. As it does this, it moves around from the ocean or other bodies of water to land. The water on land eventually flows to bodies of water again where the cycle starts over.

Now, you may be thinking, "Of course it is the water cycle. Everyone knows it exists." But here is the interesting thing. The first person to consider that rainfall played a part in global water movement was Bernard Palisy who is considered the discoverer of the modern theory of the water cycle. He lived in the late 1500s, but his ideas weren't scientifically tested until the late 1600s and weren't accepted by the scientific community until the early 1800s. Yet in verses 27-28, we see this: *For He draws up the drops of water*, which is evaporation. Then, *they distill His mist*, which is condensation. And finally, *in rain, which the skies pour down and drop on mankind abundantly* - precipitation! The entire hydrologic cycle of liquid water evaporating as gas, rising and condensing as liquid water, and then building up to precipitate back onto land or sea is scientific information that was written *thousands of years* before scientists could explain it! Where did the writer of Job get this information? He was inspired by God who is all-powerful and all-knowing. God made the universe and everything in it and set up principles so it could function - including the hydrologic cycle which is necessary for life to exist on Earth.

The Bible is filled with wisdom like this because God made the world and He knows how His world works - even when we do not!

What is God saying to me?

    It might be easy to praise God when you see His mighty works in creation, but what about during difficult times? Sometimes we are given hard assignments from God, whether it is for our personal growth or for benefits we may never completely see during our life. Romans 8:16-17 says *The Spirit Himself bears witness with our spirit that we are children of God, and if children, then heirs - heirs of God and fellow heirs with Christ, provided we suffer with Him in order that we may also be glorified with Him.* We're told that suffering is a likely part of our lives on Earth. Suffering is hard. Suffering for a purpose is possibly endurable. And suffering when we cannot see the reason behind it is a tough one. But can you see how God reveals Himself as the author of all things in this world? His wisdom is so much greater than man's wisdom (just ask Mr. Palisy who didn't figure out the hydrologic cycle nugget that God already revealed). God knows what He is doing. When we suffer, we learn patience and endurance, but we also gain a more personal perception of the fallenness of this world and a deeper desire for eternity in heaven!

    How can you give God thanks and praise when life gets challenging? Think of what Elihu said to Job in the lesson, and write your thoughts below.

What will I say to God?

If God provides us with things we require to live, such as the hydrologic cycle, won't He also provide us with the rest of our needs? Colossians 1:17 tells us He is continuously holding all of His creation in place. He upholds, He superintends, He governs His creation. He is aware of every drop of water, its location, and its movement. That means He is aware of and a part of everything that happens to you. In all things, then, we can praise His name! If you are hurting, take a walk outside or spend a moment or two looking out your window. Do you see the larger world out there? God is currently upholding you right now as He simultaneously carries the sparrow in His hand, the clouds in the sky, the moon above you, and the solar system and universe. He is fully engaged with His creation and is fully present for you. How can you praise Him today?

Day 3:

Reread the lesson's passage and dive deeper.

Look at the word, "abundantly" in verse 28. Meditate on that verse, particularly focusing on God's abundance of rain. Rain is an important, life-giving phenomenon. We hear of droughts in certain parts of the world and the challenges that come with them. Yet, sometimes we look at the rain as an inconvenience. We feel frustrated when our children's soccer game is canceled (I confess…sometimes I was happy about that). The day can feel dreary and overcast, and everything is just harder when it rains.

I remember one summer when I was in the grocery store with my four young children. As we were in the checkout lane, I heard a massive clap of thunder. There I was: a cart filled with groceries, my toddler riding in the child seat, one child sitting in the cart with the bags of food, and a child hanging onto each side of the cart. If you have that mental picture, I'm sure I don't have to mention my frustration with God at that moment. "Why did you have to make it rain now, Lord?"

Yet, from God's perspective, there is always more to the story than the little world I've created around me. Rain is necessary to keep things alive. It supports our underground water table. It is critical for watering the farmed crops that produce the food I buy at the grocery store. It even cleanses the air and the ground as it washes away the dust and pollen that would make my allergies go haywire. It is abundant in its blessing. Seeing things from God's perspective often helps me understand that what looks like a bad thing is actually for my good.

Abundance, then, is not necessarily an overflowing of the things we always want at the moments we want them. Think about that and write what abundance means to you.

Old Testament/New Testament Connection

God's Word is consistent throughout the Bible because He does not change. That means His Word is compatible between the Old Testament and the New Testament. The Old Testament verses in this week's passage focus on Job's suffering from the vantage point of God's perfect power and abundance for us. Now read the New Testament verses in Romans 8:31-39. How do the verses in Romans further develop that idea?

What is the key point of this lesson for me, and how can I apply it?

God says in His Word that He is omnipotent, creating all things and upholding all things (Job 42:1-2; Jer. 32:27; Heb. 1:3). How can the writer of Job have known about the hydrologic cycle unless he was inspired by God himself? Scientists had no idea of the cycle's existence or its importance in providing rain abundantly over the Earth. Think about what this means. Are you struggling with something and wonder if God is big enough or strong enough? Are you unsure if He is present? If He indeed upholds all things, that means his hand is ever-present, keeping all things together. What does that mean to you today?

Romans 1:18-23

¹⁸ For the wrath of God is revealed from heaven against all ungodliness and unrighteousness of men, who by their unrighteousness suppress the truth.

¹⁹ For what can be known about God is plain to them, because God has shown it to them.

²⁰ **For his invisible attributes, namely, his eternal power and divine nature, have been clearly perceived, ever since the creation of the world, in the things that have been made. So they are without excuse.**

²¹ For although they knew God, they did not honor Him as God or give thanks to Him, but they became futile in their thinking, and their foolish hearts were darkened.

²² Claiming to be wise, they became fools,

²³ and exchanged the glory of the immortal God for images resembling mortal man and birds and animals and creeping things.

1) What is the text saying? The book of Romans was written by the apostle Paul to the Christian believers in Rome. He wrote to give them practical instruction and a right understanding of the Christian way of life. Paul builds a case demonstrating that all men have sinned and all deserve God's judgment. Therefore, we all should seek *God's great, righteous rescue.* God hates sin, and all of us have sinned. But when we accept and believe that Jesus took the payment for our sins on Himself and conquered death by rising again, we take on Jesus' righteousness (Romans 3:23-24; 1 Cor. 5:21). So how do all people know that God exists, and how does God show Himself so we can know Him? God has revealed Himself in His Word and through his creation. Verse 20 tells us that God has placed evidence of Himself in the natural world around us. He has made *his eternal power and divine nature* knowable *in the things that have been made*.

2) What is the nature-truth behind the verses? Think about a sunset. One of my favorite things to do when visiting the beach is to walk down to the shore at dusk and watch the sun slowly set below the horizon. Of course, I am never alone there. I notice many other people toting beach chairs, cameras, and towels so they can watch this herald to the end of the day. That makes me think. Everyone loves a good sunset. It is beautiful, isn't it? Reds, oranges, yellows, and even purples color the sky as if it has been painted. Cell phones come out, people take silhouette-shots of themselves or they wait for a sailboat to glide by as that big yellow ball meets the water. Why do people act like that? You don't see animals doing it. Squirrels, lizards, and dolphins don't stop to observe this glorious event.

Well, first of all, think about what a sunset is. The sun isn't actually setting in relation to where we are. Rather, the Earth is spinning on its axis, and our little spot at the seashore is turning away from the sun. As we are viewing the sun when it is low in the sky, its rays of light have to travel through more of our atmosphere as compared to sun rays coming from above during the middle of the day. At sunset, the rays of light travel through more gases, water vapor, and dust particles. That causes them to refract (bend) and scatter more than they do when the sun is directly overhead. Interestingly, sunsets are often more colorful than sunrises. You see, at the end of the day, there is more dust in the air. As the sun heats the air throughout the day, the air expands and moves around, increasing wind movement and kicking up dust. Additionally, people and animals have been moving around more, stirring up material in the air for light to bend and bounce around.

So when people take time out of their day to walk outside and stare at the sky for a few minutes, think about what they are observing. Is it simply because light is bending and bouncing off of gases and dust so we can see its different wavelengths? Of course not.

We are actually beholding *more*. We aren't just looking at the physical parameters of light. Yes, there is some science-y stuff going on, but we are marveling at a sunset's *beauty*. We have the ability to identify things that are beautiful, going beyond what kinds of light waves enter our eyes. God has given us the capacity to appreciate beauty and marvel at it.

Now, whenever we see "something more" than pure science can explain, we can know that there is some One more. There is really no survival advantage to admiring a gorgeous sunset. Of the animals in the world that are able to see colors, they have no capacity to enjoy or appreciate what they're viewing.

However, people marvel at the beauty in the world because God desires us to know Him and have a relationship with Him. He has made us with the ability to see and appreciate beauty so we can enjoy God's glorious creation as it gives testimony to His greatness. An appreciation of beauty is something that cannot be explained by the science of the sunset.

That's why it is so amazing to study our world. We are beautifully made to enjoy beautiful things. Hopefully, the next time you see a sunset and start to gasp at the colors, you will think about *why* you are in awe and thank God for his beautiful creation.

What is God saying to me?

God has given you special provision to see his beauty in creation! It is important to understand that He revealed Himself both through His Word and in his glorious creation. He gave you the ability to see, hear, touch, taste, and feel it! Write what that means to you below.

What will I say to God?

Praise God for His amazing creative power - something that surpasses our understanding. Be thankful that He gives you the ability to know He is present and that He is pursuing you because He loves you. He wants you to know Him. And He gloriously paints the sky in a way that only people can see and appreciate. What are some things in nature that you consider beautiful? List some of them below. Thank God for these revelations of Himself to you. He is the author of beauty!

Day 3:
Reread the lesson's passage and dive deeper.

The main sentence of the highlighted verse is, *For His invisible attributes...have been clearly perceived...in the things that have been made.* How does our appreciation of sunsets help us to see that God's attributes are clearly perceived in His creation?

The highlighted verse also tells us exactly what His invisible attributes are: His eternal power and His divine nature. We have a hard time understanding what eternity is. Yet did you realize that, beginning from the time we are born, we are immortal? C.S. Lewis wrote, "There are no ordinary people. You have never talked to a mere mortal. Nations, cultures, arts, civilizations - they are mortal, and their life is to ours as the life of a gnat. But it is immortals whom we joke with, work with, marry, snub and exploit - immortal horrors or everlasting splendors."[1]

Did you get that last part? Immortal horrors or everlasting splendors. Unlike God who had no beginning, we were created beings with a starting date, yet from that point we will have an eternity, whether it is with Christ as *everlasting splendors* or in Sheol (the pit of the dead) as *immortal horrors*. Psalm 16:10 mentions Sheol: *For you will not abandon my soul to Sheol, or let your holy one see corruption.* Thankfully, a personal relationship with the ultimate peace-maker, Jesus - who took our sins upon Himself, bore our deserved punishment, and conquered death for us - transforms us to everlasting splendors. Read 1 Peter 1:1-11 to hear the apostle's encouragement to be *all the more diligent to confirm your calling and election*. It is an eternal issue, dear one!

Look up synonyms for the word "eternal" and prayerfully write them below as you consider your future eternal situation.

---

[1] C.S. Lewis. (1949). *The Weight of Glory*. New York, Macmillan Co. Preached originally as a sermon in the Church of St. Mary the Virgin, Oxford, on June 8, 1942.

Day 4:
Old Testament/New Testament Connection

Look at the Old Testament verses, Psalm 19:1-2. How do these verses support what is written in Romans 1:20? How does knowing those truths encourage you? How can you encourage others?

What is the key point of this lesson for me, and how can I apply it?

Take a walk outside or look closely at a painting on the wall. What beauty can you see there? Why is it beautiful? Why do you think God allows us to appreciate beautiful things, yet no other creature on Earth has that capacity? How can you share beauty with others today?

Romans 11:17-24

¹⁷ **But if some of the branches were broken off, and you, although a wild olive shoot, were grafted in among the others and now share in the nourishing root of the olive tree,**

¹⁸ do not be arrogant toward the branches. If you are, remember it is not you who support the root, but the root that supports you.

¹⁹ Then you will say, "Branches were broken off so that I might be grafted in."

²⁰ That is true. They were broken off because of their unbelief, but you stand fast through faith. So do not become proud, but fear.

²¹ For if God did not spare the natural branches, neither will He spare you.

²² Note then the kindness and the severity of God: severity toward those who have fallen, but God's kindness to you, provided you continue in His kindness. Otherwise you too will be cut off.

²³ And even they, if they do not continue in their unbelief, will be grafted in for God has the power to graft them in again.

²⁴ For if you were cut from what is by nature a wild olive tree, and grafted, contrary to nature, into a cultivated olive tree, how much more will these, the natural branches, be grafted back into their own olive tree.

1) What is the text saying? Romans is a letter written by the apostle Paul to the Christian church in Rome. In this section, Paul is warning the Gentile (non-Jewish) believers to avoid pride. That's because unbelieving Jewish "branches" were rejected, and believing Gentile "branches" were being grafted into the church. You see, this is an analogy of an olive tree, grown and nourished by God. It supports His people which are the branches. The passage mentions that some of the tree's branches were broken off, but God preserved a fragment of the tree. Now, olives were a well known crop in Paul's day, and the people understood that sometimes old olive trees would have branches that stopped producing olives. Those branches were cut or broken off, and branches from younger trees were grafted in so the tree would continue to produce a good amount of fruit. Paul referred to the Christians in Rome as those who were grafted onto the olive tree of God's people. That means they shared the blessings of God's covenant with Abraham. However, there was a danger of becoming prideful, thinking they were better than the descendants of the Jewish patriarchs. But *all* Christians are considered to be the spiritual offspring of Abraham (Gal. 3:29). Based on their belief in the finished work of Jesus, all believers will receive God's blessing and *share in the nourishing root*.

2) What is the nature-truth behind the verses? The biological analogy here is that some wild olive shoots are being grafted into an existing tree. This means the new shoots are able to get their food and water from the roots of the existing plant. Well, let's first discuss what grafting is. Once we look at this process, then we will have a better understanding of what verse 17 means for us.

Grafting is a technique where a section of a stem - called the scion (sye' ohn) - is attached to an existing tree - called the stock. It is placed onto the stock plant in such a way that the food and water transportation vessels of both pieces line up. The fancy terms for those plant vessels are xylem (zy' luhm) and phloem (flow' uhm). Xylem and phloem transport fluid and nutrients within a plant's tissues - kind of like the blood vessels in our bodies. The strings of a celery stem, for example, are its xylem and phloem. When the transport vessels of the grafted scion are lined up with the transport vessels of the stock plant, the grafted piece receives life-sustaining nutrients from the stock. In this way, the scion continues to thrive.

This grafting illustration speaks of the Gentile believers as a scion grafted into the stock of God's chosen people. They were once apart from Israel's stock, but now they have been carefully cut and placed within, able to receive God's bountiful richness and blessings.

In John 15:5, we see a similar analogy: Jesus says, I am the vine; you are the branches. Whoever abides in me and I in Him, he it is that bears much fruit, for apart from me you can do nothing. We as believers are grafted into the body of Christ, receiving the blessings promised to His universal church. All of our nourishment, then, is provided by the main root. We are all a part of the same plant.

This gives us a great opportunity to think about how we live with one another. You see, as Christians, we are not each other's enemy. We each have special fruit we produce. Continuing the biblical analogy, some of us may make green olives while others make black ones. Yet if we work against one another, we interfere with the other branches' abilities to gain nutrients or sunlight, slowing their growth. We might think that if they are not making the same kind of olives that we are, they must be doing it wrong. That type of thinking can make us want to grow over them, blocking their sunlight, choking them off.

That is not our purpose. As believers we are brothers and sisters in Christ, all connected to the life-giving root of the olive tree. We all receive nourishment from God's Word and life-giving peace through Jesus. We are then able to grow and produce great fruit - fruit that is unique to the way we are made! Because each grafted branch produces unique olive fruits simultaneously, we as the body of Christ produce a cornucopia of spiritual fruit, serving others, spreading the gospel, and bringing the hope of God's gospel to a dry and hungry world!

What is God saying to me?

There are many things that can divide us within the church: topics such as politics, parenting methods, and even what we do and do not eat! However, most of these topics are side issues that should not separate us. Indeed, there are things on which we should all agree: there is one way of salvation in Christ, there are things that the Bible calls sin, etc. But it's important to remember that the Bride of Christ is made up of all believers, representing different cultures and languages and who might live life in a different way than we do. Considering the grafting analogy, you can think of the body of Christ - the Church - as one single body just as if it was a single olive tree. When we focus on peripheral issues that cause our "leaves" to cover over each other, we create bigger problems. How can you re-frame your mind and heart to see other Christians who might be different from you as being a part of the same family?

Day 2:
What will I say to God?

What happens if one part of the tree covers over another part so that it cannot see the sun? Sadly, that happens often in Christian circles. Our churches can become places where we tend to create exclusive groups, making it difficult for others to enter in. Yes, my friends, the cliques that many of us experienced as teens have not disappeared. They may be in your church right now. Cliques can do great damage to other believers and to the greater body of Christ. Think about that analogy and ask God to help you understand the importance of embracing believers who might be different. Does an outsider feel welcome when they visit your church? Ask God for eyes to see others in a loving way. And remember that you, too, were once outside the tree. Thank God for grafting you into the olive tree so you can receive the rich blessings He has for you. Write any thoughts you have about this below.

Reread the lesson's passage and dive deeper.

The highlighted verse mentions that the wild olive shoots were grafted in to the olive tree to share in the nourishing root. With a clearer understanding of the grafting process, think about what this verse means to you regarding your identity.

Now read Gal. 3:26-29. *For in Christ Jesus you are all sons of God, through faith. For as many of you as were baptized into Christ have put on Christ. There is neither Jew nor Greek, there is neither slave nor free, there is no male and female, for you are all one in Christ Jesus. And if you are Christ's, then you are Abraham's offspring, heirs according to promise.* How does this verse relate to the passage in Romans?

_____

_____

_____

What is my identity? That is a tough one. Personally, I can give myself lots of titles: wife, mom, friend, sister, Christian, science nerd, and more. But are those things the sum of me? I'm also a part of various friend, family, and church groups. And those groups also furnish me with an identity of who I am - I belong to those groups. However, the Galatians passage says there is no Jew nor Greek, slave nor free. Do we join the body of Christ and become homogeneous?

Am I giving up my me-ness to be a "we"? In reality, we're not called to throw away our uniqueness when entering the body. Being brought into union with Jesus by faith is to be with other believers in love. So our identities aren't a mash-up of all our existences. The new "we" is shaped by Christ, so we're in the world, but we're now influenced by different eyes and a different mind. New lenses to see the same world. Death to the old self and life to the new self. We have new lives in a real world with a new reality. Col. 1:26 speaks of *the mystery hidden for ages and generations but now revealed to his saints...* Christ in us! We are a community that God is creating, each bringing his or her own uniqueness, but all of us putting off our earthly unpleasantness (a nice way to put it!) and putting on compassion (Col. 3:7-17). This is the church the world should see.

How does that affect your thoughts about who you are as a grafted part of the olive tree...as a part of Christ's universal church?

_____

_____

_____

#

Old Testament/New Testament Connection

Read Is. 56:6-8. *And the foreigners who join themselves to the Lord, to minister to Him, to love the name of the Lord, and to be His servants, everyone who keeps the Sabbath and does not profane it, and holds fast my covenant - these I will bring to my holy mountain, and make them joyful in my house of prayer; their burnt offerings and their sacrifices will be accepted on my altar; for my house shall be called a house of prayer for all peoples. The Lord God, who gathers the outcasts of Israel, declares, "I will gather yet others to Him besides those already gathered."*

Long before Jesus took our sins on the cross and paid the debt we owe, the Old Testament writers mentioned how foreigners would be brought into the house of Israel. This was all part of God's plan.

How does that relate to being grafted into one tree? Can you see how it is God's intention that all believers should be united in Christ? 1 Peter 1:22 says, *Having purified your souls by your obedience to the truth for a sincere brotherly love, love one another earnestly from a pure heart.* Reflect and pray on these words.

What is the key point of this lesson for me, and how can I apply it?

The Enemy is having a field day as he works to break up our families and the greater Church. 1 Peter 5:8 says, *Be sober-minded; be watchful. Your adversary the devil prowls around like a roaring lion, seeking someone to devour.* Can you think of any broken relationship you might have with fellow believers? Remember you are a part of the same tree. You are both receiving the nourishment of the Word of God and you share the same roots!

1 John 3:1-3 says, *See what kind of love the Father has given to us, that we should be called children of God; and so we are. The reason why the world does not know us is that it did not know Him. Beloved, we are God's children now, and what we will be has not yet appeared; but we know that when He appears we shall be like Him, because we shall see Him as He is. And everyone who thus hopes in Him purifies himself as He is pure.*

Don't let Satan take away your peace. Reflect on the verses above and pray, asking God to show you what you can do to begin reconciliation. Make the first move toward your brother or sister in Christ. And do it with patience and love - for the strength of the whole tree!

Week 4:

The Fear of the Lord is Wisdom - Earth's Atmosphere
Read Job 28:23-28

Job 28:23-28

²³ *God understands the way to it, and He knows its place.*

²⁴ *For He looks to the ends of the earth and sees everything under the heavens.*

²⁵ **When He gave to the wind its weight** *and apportioned the waters by measure,*

²⁶ *when He made a decree for the rain and a way for the lightning of the thunder,*

²⁷ *then He saw it and declared it; He established it, and searched it out.*

²⁸ *And He said to man, 'Behold, the fear of the Lord, that is wisdom, and to turn away from evil is understanding.'*

1) What is the text saying? In this passage, Job is speaking to his friends who have been trying to determine why Job is experiencing suffering. He talks about the treasures of Earth and reminds them that the wisdom needed to understand his situation is not something people can easily grasp. Only God can know it, because God knows everything and has true wisdom. Although we cannot fully understand the mind of God, we do know that to be wise is to be in awe of God and to trust Him (v. 28). We may never understand why there are times of suffering in life because we don't have an eternal vantage point. However, we can trust and obey God and His Word - His truth for us!

2) What is the nature-truth behind the verse? The highlighted verse says the wind has weight. Now, during Job's day people thought air was not made of anything. So that statement should have been a surprise to the readers of his text. The first known scholar to even mention that air was made of "stuff" was Aristotle, but this was 300 years B.C. (long after Job's time) and he had no scientific evidence to support that idea. It wasn't until 1644 A.D. that Evangelista Torricelli was able to accurately measure air's mass, meaning air (and the wind) has weight.[2]

So scientists discovered that the wind had weight in the 1600s, yet this fact was already detailed in Job over 4,000 years ago! This is no small point, my friends, because the air in our atmosphere has many important jobs. We need the air to be made of material, and it has to be a perfect mix of material for us to survive. God made it for us.

---

[2] West, J.B. (2013). Torricelli and the ocean of air: The first measurement of barometric pressure. *Physiology (Bethesda, Md.), 28*(2), 66-73. https://doi.org/10.1152/physiol.00053.2012

What do I mean? Well, our sun produces just the right amount of sunlight for living things to survive on Earth. But part of that light contains harmful rays, such as ultraviolet rays, x-rays, and gamma rays. These rays carry an extreme amount of solar energy that can kill living cells. So why aren't we being fried to pieces right now? Simple. These three attackers to our Earth are protected by exactly three perfect lines of defense, specifically by an atmosphere (air) with just the right gases in just the right amounts.

Most of our air is made of nitrogen gas which specifically blocks deadly gamma rays that would damage living tissue. Destructive x-rays are blocked by the oxygen gas in our atmosphere. And harmful ultraviolet rays (the ones we are always warned about when going out in the sun) are stopped by a third key gas in our atmosphere: ozone.

The more we learn about our weighty wind the more we see God's intentional design. And here is another fascinating point: ozone is poisonous to living things. So it is not mixed in with the rest of the air we breathe in large quantities. Instead, it "just happens" to be located in an atmospheric layer above where life exists. Isn't that amazing? We need ozone to protect our Earth, but we can't have it where we are living. So instead of being evenly mixed with the other gases in our atmosphere, most ozone exists high above us, yet still within the Earth's protective atmospheric blanket. Thus, not only do the gases have to be present, they must exist in just the right concentrations and in the perfect locations for life to exist.

Now we can get back to Job's mention of how God gave the wind its weight. When we understand that this was a scientifically accurate statement made before anyone knew that air was made of material and that the special material in our atmosphere has critical life-giving purpose, we can see how God's Word is true. There is no accident in His creation of the universe, the world, and of YOU!

What is God saying to me?

Think about how the writer of Job knew that air had weight and what that says about the wisdom of God. How should we respond when things happen in life that we don't understand? Will we be in awe of Him because of His creation and power? Will we trust in His wisdom and obey His Word?

Day 2:
What will I say to God?

Ask God for wisdom when you pray. Ask Him to reveal truths in His Word and help you see His creative hand in the world around you. Although we may not understand a specific circumstance, we can tell God we know He is the creator of everything and we can be in awe of Him, trusting His perfect purposes.

Think about any Bible passages that might be hard for you to comprehend. You might struggle with the idea of God permitting suffering in the world or allowing a person's heart to be hardened. Yet, we do not know the mind of God. When we see nature-truths like the one in this passage, we can remember that God knows what we do not know. God sees what we do not see. God is outside of time and has a perspective we cannot have. Oh, these can be hard things to struggle with! What do we do with them? We call out to our wise and loving creator-God, asking Him to build our trust in Him.

Reread the lesson's passage and dive deeper.

These words in Job chronicle what the Lord did when He established the world. They are meant for Job and for us today to understand the magnitude of God's power in creation. Yet they reveal more. Re-read the passage and focus on the key words in verse 27: *declared, established, searched*. Then consider those words in light of verse 28 when God said to man, "*Behold, the fear of the Lord, that is wisdom.*" What does that mean to you?

Old Testament/New Testament Connection

Read 1 Peter 1:13-19. In this passage, Peter encourages the believers in a calling to be holy. One of those exhortations is to *conduct yourselves with fear* (v.17). Our passage in Job says, *behold, the fear of the Lord, that is wisdom.* Meditate on those words today and consider the connection between the fear of the Lord and wisdom in light of the words in 1 Peter that tell us to conduct ourselves with fear.

What is the key point of this lesson for me, and how can I apply it?

In the Bible, God graciously reveals the way our world is established and how it works. Many times, great knowledge is given...knowledge that science has not even explored or understood. And that should be expected. The author of the universe spoke all of creation into being. That means His Word is filled with truth and wisdom. Write out Job 28:28 below and then memorize it so that you can always be encouraged by its words.

Job 28:28 *And He said to man, 'Behold, the fear of the Lord, that is wisdom, and to turn away from evil is understanding.'*

Psalm 103:1-14

¹ *Bless the Lord, O my soul, and all that is within me, bless His holy name!*

² *Bless the Lord, O my soul, and forget not all His benefits,*

³ *who forgives all your iniquity, who heals all your diseases,*

⁴ *who redeems your life from the pit, who crowns you with steadfast love and mercy,*

⁵ *who satisfies you with good so that your youth is renewed like the eagle's.*

⁶ *The Lord works righteousness and justice for all who are oppressed.*

⁷ *He made known His ways to Moses, His acts to the people of Israel.*

⁸ *The Lord is merciful and gracious, slow to anger and abounding in steadfast love.*

⁹ *He will not always chide, nor will He keep His anger forever.*

¹⁰ *He does not deal with us according to our sins, nor repay us according to our iniquities.*

¹¹ **For as high as the heavens are above the earth, so great is His steadfast love toward those who fear Him;**

¹² **as far as the east is from the west, so far does He remove our transgressions from us.**

¹³ *As a father shows compassion to His children, so the Lord shows compassion to those who fear Him.*

¹⁴ *For He knows our frame; He remembers that we are dust.*

1) What is the text saying? Psalm 103 is a psalm of praise to God. It focuses on His great characteristics and what He has done for us, including His forgiveness (saving us from the consequences of our sin) and redemption (brought back, free to live for Him). People will often praise God after winning a great battle or recovering from a tragedy. But this psalm doesn't mention that it was written after any historic event. Instead, it is more of a timeless psalm - one of praise by those who fear the Lord (vv. 11 and 13). Now, when people worship God it becomes richer and deeper the more they know Him. So if you don't know much about God's awesome qualities and great works and you don't spend regular time with Him (in His Word and through prayer), then it will be hard to sincerely praise Him.

The writer of this psalm is praising God for His glory and the grace He has given to rescue us. Look at verse 2. It says, *forget not all His benefits*. Those benefits are His great goodness to us including everything He has done in creation and every merciful thing

He has done for us. The next verses then list many of those specific benefits. In fact, this entire psalm encourages us to continually remember the Lord's benefits to us. Think about what He has done for you today alone. Today you have been forgiven, protected, encouraged, instructed, and blessed! Doesn't that make your heart overflow with praise to God? Even though He is a just God and we deserve great punishment for our sins, He has shown us great mercy and grace because His son Jesus took the punishment for our sins in our place. He has separated our sins from us. How far? Well, how high can you count? It's even further than that - the separation is so great that it goes to infinity.

2) What is the nature-truth behind the verses? A major point in this praise-filled psalm has to do with God's greatest gift to His people - the forgiveness of sins (v.3). We live in New Testament times today, so we have even greater revelation of what the forgiveness of sins means. In the Old Testament, people looked ahead to the coming Savior, but today we look behind at the work of Jesus, our Savior who took the punishment of our sins on Himself and conquered death for those who believe. That is our greatest joy. Many people spend their lives trying to reach the goal of a perfect job, a prestigious status, or a filled bank account. Sadly, when those goals are reached, most people realize those are not fulfilling in themselves; they are just not satisfying. That's because we were created for more. When we receive forgiveness for our sins, we then get to spend today, tomorrow, and all of eternity with our God! Being with God is something that fills the deepest need we have, and it can never be taken away from us. How great is this forgiveness that results in such a relationship with God? Well, it is illustrated by two examples of infinity.

Infinity is a value that represents something with no end or boundaries. In a numerical example, infinity goes beyond what we can count. No matter how large a number you count to, you can always add one more - infinity has no end. God's gracious loving kindness for us is so great that verse 11 says it's *as high as the heavens are above the Earth*. Well, how high are the heavens from Earth? So far, we have not even come close to knowing. Scientists only have estimates to where the edges of our universe are. In fact, if we were to travel at the speed of light it would take over *200 trillion years* to get even close to where scientists *think* the outer edges are. This illustration means God's love for His people is boundless - to infinity.

The second infinity illustration is in verse 12 when believers are told how far their sins are removed from them. If you trust Jesus as your Savior, your sins are separated from you *as far as the east is from the west*. How far is that, and why didn't it say as far as the north is from the south? Well, think about it. If you start to travel north, eventually you will reach the northernmost point on the planet - near the North Pole. Then if you continue in a straight line, you will no longer be moving north anymore, but rather you'll be moving south. The same thing happens if you start traveling south; eventually you will be going north again. There is a definite, measurable distance between north and south (approximately 12,440 miles on Earth). However, if you were to travel in an easterly direction, you could always keep moving toward the east, couldn't you? There is no boundary to stop you. No matter where you are in your travels, you can always face east and continue. So the distance between east and west is infinite! That infinite forgiveness is explained in verse 13 when it compares a father's compassion on his children to the Lord's compassion on those who fear Him. He knows us. He is our Father and He loves us even better than any earthly father could. And when we see the infinite extent to which He declares His forgiveness and His love, we have much to praise Him for!

What is God saying to me?

God loves you, perfectly and completely. At this very moment he is protecting you, encouraging you, and teaching you. God has given you true salvation in the completed work of Jesus and has separated your sins from you, farther than you can imagine. So when He looks at you, He sees no sin but rather the shed blood and perfect obedience of Jesus. Do you believe this? What can you do to remind yourself that His Word is true? How can you share that good news with others?

What will I say to God?

After reading this psalm, how can you praise God for His great works? One way is to read the words in the psalm back to God in prayer. For example, if you pray verse 8 to God you might say, "Lord you are merciful and gracious. You do not become angry quickly and you love me continually. I praise you!" Pray through this psalm today and then write down anything that brought you encouragement.

Re-read the lesson's passage and dive deeper.

It can be difficult to think of the attributes of God. After all, our natural inclinations can only imagine a God like us. We cannot comprehend His true, infinite magnitude; He is both mighty and gentle, righteous and forgiving. Because we are living within the constraints of time, our minds struggle with imagining things beyond the finite and the earthly. Yet when we study the God who is revealed to us in the Bible, we can break down those preconceived ideas. There, we are faced with the infinite perfection of our Lord and the infinite forgiveness we get through His son, Jesus. There is infinite power in the triune God, yet there is also infinite gentleness. Jesus Himself gives us a glimpse of that in Matthew 11:28-30.

Come to me, all who labor and are heavy laden, and I will give you rest. Take my yoke upon you, and learn from me, for I am gentle and lowly in heart, and you will find rest for your souls. For my yoke is easy, and my burden is light.

God's steadfast love for us is as high as the heavens are from the Earth. His ability to forgive and forget our sinful nature based on the finished work of Jesus is infinite.

Look at verses 3-5 on this lesson's passage. They have to do with the benefits of the Lord as mentioned in verse 2. The action verbs from those verses are listed below. Read them in the context of the verses and reflect on how they each exhibit a characteristic of God *for* you.

Forgives

Heals

Redeems

Crowns

Satisfies

Day 4:
Old Testament/New Testament Connection

Read Colossians 3:12-13: *Put on then, as God's chosen ones, holy and beloved, compassionate hearts, kindness, humility, meekness, and patience, bearing with one another and, if one has a complaint against another, forgiving each other; as the Lord has forgiven you, so you also must forgive.*

Think about those verses. As God's chosen ones, you are loved and forgiven.

I often struggled with that. When my children were younger and the days were filled with character building (Who am I kidding? Let's just call it what it was...stopping the screaming and bickering and training them to get along with one another), I found myself constantly having to hold my tongue, reign in my temper, and hold off feelings of selfishness because I felt like everyone kept needing me for everything and I never had time for myself.

I constantly spent the few moments of quiet time I had asking God for forgiveness of wrong attitudes. It got so bad that I really couldn't believe that I was truly forgiven for it all. I mean, how many "get out of jail free" cards were there for me? Did I use up all my credits yet?

But God doesn't operate like that. Jesus' blood covers ALL my sins...ALL. It's hard for me to believe that, because I "know" me. The older I get and the more I know about God, the greater I realize the depths of my sins. Can they truly be forgiven to infinity?

Look over the highlighted verse in the lesson's passage and the verses above in Colossians. How do they relate to one another? How do these truths address any doubt you have about being loved and forgiven?

Day 5:

What is the key point of this lesson for me, and how can I apply it?

Isn't it amazing how God's attributes do not change throughout the Bible? He is truly the unchanging God! As high as the heavens are from the Earth, you are loved! As far as the east is from the west, your sins are removed from you. It's infinity! Knowing that you are wholly loved and completely forgiven, how does that change what you will do today? How does that bring peace to your heart? Can you allow yourself to rest in those words?

Psalm 119:97-104

⁹⁷ Oh how I love your law, it is my meditation all the day.

⁹⁸ Your commandment makes me wiser than my enemies, for it is ever with me.

⁹⁹ I have more understanding than all my teachers, for your testimonies are my meditation.

¹⁰⁰ I understand more than the aged, for I keep your precepts.

¹⁰¹ I hold back my feet from every evil way, in order to keep your word.

¹⁰² I do not turn aside from your rules, for you have taught me.

¹⁰³ **How sweet are your words to my taste, sweeter than honey to my mouth!**

¹⁰⁴ Through your precepts I get understanding; therefore I hate every false way.

1) What is the text saying? Psalm 119 is believed to have been written by king David, the prophet Daniel, or the prophet Ezra. This psalm is the longest chapter in the book of Psalms (even longer than some *entire* books of the Bible) and it is divided into groups of eight verses, each group representing a letter of the Hebrew alphabet. That is why the Hebrew letter and the word *Mem* are at the beginning of our Bible text today. *Mem* is the thirteenth letter of the Hebrew alphabet. This section of the Psalm begins with David expressing His love for God's law. He loved God's law so much that he meditated on it, studying it and reading it again and again. Have you ever received a letter or card from someone that really made you feel great? You likely read it over and over. That is a type of meditation. But when we read the Bible, there is often much deeper meaning that God has for us besides just making us feel great. His commandments are wise for us to follow.

When you get an instruction manual for a product you purchase, the manual gives you directions for how it works and ways to properly use it. Well, God's Word is written FOR us. It is our instruction manual for living. Romans 15:4 says, *For whatever was written in former days was written for our instruction, that through endurance and through the encouragement of the Scriptures we might have hope.* God's Word is filled with His wisdom, and it is delightful to read. It is tasty. David's pleasure and delight in God's Word was clear as he described it as sweeter than honey (v. 103), a food that in his day was the ultimate dessert! He was saying that the Word of God was sweeter than any satisfaction of taste we could ever have.

2) What is the nature-truth behind the verses? Think about our focus verse. Why did God give us the ability to taste food? Some might say it was to keep us from eating things that are harmful to us, such as poisonous mushrooms or spoiled cheese. That's because bitter or sour tastes might indicate something could be bad for us, while sweet and salty tastes would signal food is rich in nutrients and good to eat. But the extensive *range* of our taste buds gives us a clue that there is something more. We only require a narrow spectrum of taste receptors to identify good food from bad food. Yet the complexity of our sense of taste points to the extraordinary reality that we were made to experience something greater.

Scientists are learning that our sense of taste is much more complicated than the five basic factors of sweet, salty, sour, bitter, and savory. Taste buds are complex organs made of many sensory cells connected to nerves. When you eat something, the food chemicals come in contact with those sensory cells, causing signals to be sent along nerve fibers to your brain. Then your brain processes that electrical information to identify a flavor.

Yet flavors are more complicated than sweet or salty alone. Most are a result of a combination of many of our taste buds firing simultaneously. When you bite into a slice of pizza, for example, you are getting salty flavors from the cheese, sweet from the tomato sauce, savory from pepperoni and garlic, and sour from the tomato acids. Plus, these sensory cells can identify about ten levels of intensity for each flavor, such as the difference between slightly sweet and very sweet. Spicy flavors are actually a result of pain signals in your mouth. If you enjoy spicy foods, your brain associates those mild pain signals as something fun – like screaming while you're riding a roller-coaster. Add to that the smell of the baked bread, texture of the crust, gooey-ness of the cheese, and the warmth of the slice, and you have a complete symphony in a mouthful! So all these flavor types, intensities, pain levels, smells, textures, and temperatures mean that our brain can identify millions of different tastes. If our sense of taste was simply to tell the difference between poisonous and safe food, then these complex sensations are way more than what we need.

Why do we have such a diverse sense of taste? Well, we often connect taste with how we feel. Flavors such as bitter or sweet connect with the emotions of sadness or joy. The science of taste is just now catching up with these ideas. Indeed, verse 103 says, *How sweet are your words to my taste, sweeter than honey to my mouth*! So God gave us our tasting ability to not only identify what is safe or unsafe to eat but also for our enjoyment of His great creation and to better communicate the complex feelings and experiences we have. God's Word, then, is something we can taste and savor!

Day 1:
What is God saying to me?

Do you truly appreciate God's Word? Well, how often do you actually read it? Do you just open your Bible during church, or do you set aside time each day to seek the wisdom that is there for you? God invites us to know and experience Him by listening to what He has to say to us in His Word. Do you think about the Bible as tasty nourishment that is sweeter than honey? How can you intentionally make time to read and meditate on God's wisdom?

What will I say to God?

One great revelation I had when I first started reading the Bible was how it was living. I don't mean that the book had a heart and muscles and was "alive." Rather, it was more than just words on a page. For example, I would read through a New Testament book and as I read it, I noticed things that were helpful or encouraging to me. I kept a notebook so I could write down my thoughts and what I prayed about at that time. But later – sometimes a year or two later – when I started reading that same book, I noticed completely different things. That was because I was going through a different season in life compared to the first time I read it. Yet those words were just as applicable and relevant. They had something to say to me *right where I was*. They came alive in my heart!

Have you ever read a verse that you've read before, but this time it had a different application for you? That is one thing that is unique about the living Word of God. Hebrews 4:12 says *For the Word of God is living and active, sharper than any two-edged sword, piercing to the division of soul and of spirit, of joints and of marrow, and discerning the thoughts and intentions of the heart.*

Ask God to help you "love His Word like delicious food." Ask for understanding and wisdom as you read His Word. Remind yourself that His Words are full of truths to discover and learn more about each day.

#

Reread the lesson's passage and dive deeper.

The highlighted verse talks of God's Word being so sweet to taste, even sweeter than anything else in the world. Let's take that analogy one step further and talk about the nourishment that comes from reading the Word of God. Nourishment for our bodies has to do with taking in food and other materials that our bodies require for growth and health. So the nourishment from God's Word is food for our soul, providing what we need to thrive. It makes us whole when we are broken, transforms our weakness into strength, and heals our hurts. Read Matthew 4:3-4 when Jesus was tempted by Satan in the desert. What did Jesus say about the nourishment of the Word of God?

Day 4:
Old Testament/New Testament Connection

Think about the importance of reading God's Word. Look up the following verses and write what they show you.

Romans 15:4
2 Timothy 3:16
John 8:31
John 20:31
Mark 13:31

What is the key point of this lesson for me, and how can I apply it?

Do you want to hunger for God's Word the same way you hunger for food? Sometimes it can be difficult, because the verses we read may not sound so tasty to us. They actually might "bite back" as they point out our sinful struggles. But you can view the instructions in the Bible as spiritual nutrients that will make your spiritual life more healthful. Ask God to give you a true hunger for the healthful Word. Write out your prayer below.

Week 7:

God's Timeline For Us - Dormancy
Read Ecclesiastes 3:1-8

Ecclesiastes 3:1-8

¹ **For everything there is a season, and a time for every matter under heaven:**

² *a time to be born, and a time to die; a time to plant, and a time to pluck up what is planted;*

³ *a time to kill, and a time to heal; a time to break down, and a time to build up;*

⁴ *a time to weep, and a time to laugh; a time to mourn, and a time to dance;*

⁵ *a time to cast away stones, and a time to gather stones together; a time to embrace, and a time to refrain from embracing;*

⁶ *a time to seek, and a time to lose; a time to keep, and a time to cast away;*

⁷ *a time to tear, and a time to sew; a time to keep silence, and a time to speak;*

⁸ *a time to love, and a time to hate; a time for war, and a time for peace.*

1) What is the text saying? The book of Ecclesiastes is believed to be written by King Solomon, King David's son. He was writing to his people to inspire them to live their lives by God's wisdom, not by their own wisdom (Eccl. 12:13). He instructed them that God's created world was set up with appointed times for things to occur. You already know that while we live on Earth, there will be a passing of time. All living things grow, mature, and get older until they pass away.

Additionally, we have very little control over what happens to us in our lives. We can work hard, we can eat healthfully, and yet there will be storms and sickness, too. So if we live our lives with a desire to control them, we will eventually become frustrated, won't we? We cannot control life, so we should not try to. Instead, the author tells us that we should open our hands out to the Lord, knowing that He *does* control all things and has a beautiful purpose in all His works. Eccl. 12:13 sums it all up by saying what we should do: *fear God and keep His commandments, for this is the whole duty of man.*

Now, we *do* have control over some things, don't we? For example, we can control our *attitude*. So during times of sadness and loss, we don't have to worry because we know God is in control. He uses even what might look like bad things for good purposes. Your life is extremely important because God has a perfect plan for you. You might not see immediate answers to your prayers or solutions to your problems, but in God's perfect timing all things will happen according to His plan and for your good (Rom. 8:28).

2) What is the nature-truth behind the verses? You know that the seasons change as each year passes. Winter months eventually give rise to springtime. Then spring passes to summer. Finally, summer ends and autumn begins, wrapping up the calendar year with winter again. Well, let's talk more about our highlighted verse which states that for everything there is a season or a specific time.

Many people have a favorite season of the year. And many also have a season they would prefer to skip. If you live in northern areas, the winter months can drag slowly by, particularly once the holiday season ends. In the South, the seemingly endless summer heat can be exhausting. However all seasons are important. The spring and summer seasons are warm times when fresh fruits are ripe and daylight hours are long. Plants grow wildly as the sun and rain provide the components they need to make food. In the fall and winter, plants slow their growth. Many trees lose their leaves, making them appear dead. Yet, the trees are not dead at all. They become dormant.

But the winter dormant season is not a stagnant time. Rather, it is a time of preparation. You see, although growth slows, things are still very active on the inside. Times of dormancy are actually vibrant, because internal growth is happening. Grasses, bushes, and trees are preparing inside for warmer spring weather when they will sprout, bud, and bloom! Indeed, *there is a time for every matter under heaven*, even dormancy.

Day 1:
What is God saying to me?

Just like the seasons cycle through times of apparent barrenness, we can go through "spiritually" dormant winters. We can feel like God is being silent in our lives. There is no progress or future in sight. Life just doesn't seem exciting, and from the outside we might feel that we are spiritually dead. But that doesn't mean things are stagnant. Remember, God is always upholding us and transforming us, making us more like Him. You see, as God works to conform us to Himself, we'll experience lots of internal, spiritual growth in order to be prepared for what He has for us in the future. He has an eternal plan for us, as well as a moment-by-moment plan. And part of that involves transforming us. Romans 12:2 says, *Do not be conformed to this world, but be transformed by the renewal of your mind, that by testing you may discern what is the will of God, what is good and acceptable and perfect.* The transformation includes developing our inner character. Are you surprised to know that times of stillness and seeming stagnancy are actually character-building times when we are being prepared for upcoming growth? Is that counter-intuitive? How does that fact change your outlook on dormant seasons of life?

Day 2:
What will I say to God?

I remember a time when my father was very ill. He had a history of heart problems, and his health was failing. This coincided with a very busy parenting season for my husband and me. Our children were in their high school years. Some were dual-enrolled in our local community college and taking rigorous classes. Others were on sports teams and had practices and games. This was a season filled with carpools, part-time jobs, and outside social activities. Yet among my siblings, I was the only one living in town with my father. He had many needs as his health began to decline. One year in particular, we moved him into our home, then back out to his apartment, then to the hospital, to the rehab facility, back to us, and back to his apartment. Each move required lots of paperwork, packing and unpacking of his things, and lots of other responsibilities. I was grateful I could be there for him, but I really felt like I was dropping the ball with my family.

Dear friends stepped up with offers to drive our kids to events, bring us meals, and lots more. Now, we homeschooled our children. During that season, I felt like we had lost an entire year of education because of the extra pull on my time. But God worked through that season, growing my trust in Him, blessing me with increased time with my father (who passed away a few months later), and building in my children a sense of responsibility. It also demonstrated to us the extended love of our church family. And our children's end-of-year assessments showed that they were learning well above where they needed to be! That hard season was definitely not fun, and I didn't feel like I was experiencing any growth – I looked like a mess, just barely getting by. But once I could step back and look at that season with new perspective, I saw how God was truly using it to grow me closer to Him.

During your life you will likely experience times of sadness, hurt, and challenges. Illness, job-loss, and friend or family struggles all can play a part in this. It can be hard to identify any progress, and it might even feel like God is not present. But that is the most critical time to keep moving forward, reading God's Word, and spending time with Him in prayer. That's because challenging times help us remember that we do not have control of things. We can feel like those leafless trees in winter. Stagnant. Brown. Dormant. Seemingly existing, with no visible growth. But we can call out to our Lord. We can express our hurts and we can ask Him to show us what He is doing *in us* through these difficulties. Write your thoughts about that below.

_____

_____

Reread the lesson's passage and dive deeper.

Today's passage is filled with opposites. Review the verses and write them down: born-die; plant-pluck, etc. What does this tell you about the timing of all these things? Do most of them happen all at once or are they experiences that happen over a lifetime? There is a natural peace that comes from reviewing a person's experiences over decades of living an ordinary life. In fact, the ordinary experiences of life show us the extraordinary that happened in those simple events. A life well-lived doesn't necessarily have glitz and glamour but it always has times of joy and sorrow, ease and hardship. It is how we walk through those times that is important. The ups are easy to walk *through*, but the downs… well…the downs are just plain harder, aren't they? How do these verses encourage you when it comes time for the dormant seasons of life?

Day 4:
Old Testament/New Testament Connection

Read the following verses:

Phil. 1:6 *And I am sure of this, that He who began a good work in you will bring it to completion at the day of Jesus Christ.*

Heb. 12:11 *For the moment all discipline seems painful rather than pleasant, but later it yields the peaceful fruit of righteousness to those who have been trained by it.*

How do the above verses tie in with the highlighted verse in Ecclesiastes?

Day 5:

What is the key point of this lesson for me, and how can I apply it?

Someone once said that it is a certainty in life that things are not certain. That may be true from our perspective, but it is not true from God's perspective. He has purpose in all that happens, which means we can faithfully walk through all seasons of life. During times of dormancy, we do what the trees do. We take in the nutrients we need to be ready for the "blooming" God has for us ahead. We build solid habits of spending time with Him, reading His Word, and reminding ourselves that God has great plans for us. Times of dormancy, then, are times to prepare. This involves discipline and consistency. Daily doing the next thing set before you. It may not look exciting. It may even look boring. But know that God has amazing plans for your life. He desires you to be fulfilled in Him. He is working to transform you into a beautiful creation. So though you may be feeling dormant, know that this is a time for internal growth. God is indeed building and strengthening you inside! What are practical ways to build yourself during dormant times? How can you be present for others who are experiencing times of dormancy?

Proverbs 25:11-20

¹¹ *A word fitly spoken is like apples of gold in a setting of silver.*

¹² *Like a gold ring or an ornament of gold is a wise reprover to a listening ear.*

¹³ *Like the cold of snow in the time of harvest is a faithful messenger to those who send him; he refreshes the soul of his masters.*

¹⁴ *Like clouds and wind without rain is a man who boasts of a gift he does not give.*

¹⁵ *With patience a ruler may be persuaded, and a soft tongue will break a bone.*

¹⁶ *If you have found honey, eat only enough for you, lest you have your fill of it and vomit it.*

¹⁷ *Let your foot be seldom in your neighbor's house, lest he have his fill of you and hate you.*

¹⁸ *A man who bears false witness against his neighbor is like a war club, or a sword, or a sharp arrow.*

¹⁹ *Trusting in a treacherous man in time of trouble is like a bad tooth or a foot that slips.*

²⁰ **Whoever sings songs to a heavy heart is like one who takes off a garment on a cold day, and like vinegar on soda.**

1) What is the text saying? The book of Proverbs is primarily authored by King Solomon (King David's son). Chapter 25 begins a collection of over 100 proverbs spoken by him. They were compiled by Hezekiah, king of Judah (Prov. 25:1) and were intended to remind the people in his kingdom about Solomon's great wisdom. Interestingly, many of the verses in both Chapters 25 and 26 include similes. For example, verse 14 compares clouds and wind that promise rain but do not produce it to a man who promises a gift but does not give it. They are intended as visible ways for us to understand God's wisdom for how we should live. The Proverbs are great instruction for us because they skillfully apply the truths and principles of God's law in a practical way. Many of the verses here urge us to love others well. We are encouraged to speak winsomely and truthfully (verses 11, 14, and 18), inspire others to keep from sinning (verse 12), speak gently (verse 15), behave considerately and with self-control (verses 16 and 17), and be wary of unreliable people (verse 19).

2) What is the nature-truth behind the verses? Our highlighted verse is also a simile, comparing a person who sings happy songs when someone is very sad to a person who takes off a coat when it is cold or when vinegar is mixed with soda. You already know that taking off your coat when it's cold makes you feel colder. It just makes you feel worse, right? Well, singing happy songs to someone who is feeling very sad will make them feel even sadder. So why does Solomon add another simile by mentioning vinegar and soda? He does it to give us a visual image of what that feels like. You see, soda refers to a group of materials such as saltpeter (made of potassium nitrate – KNO_3), lime (which is basically calcium oxide – CaO), or sodium bicarbonate (which is baking soda – $NaHCO_3$). When any of these are added to vinegar in the right combinations, the mixture can be explosive! You've probably safely mixed baking soda and vinegar when you were in school or with your children. That combination is often used as part of a volcano experiment, and the bubbling-over is quite memorable, isn't it?

The two compounds chemically react because baking soda is a base and vinegar is an acid. When acids and bases are mixed together, a violent reaction often results, producing new chemicals. When vinegar and soda react together, carbon dioxide gas forms as bubbles, and just like the bubbles in a carbonated drink, the gas bubbles up to form an eruptive foam!

Now, let's get back to our key verse. Thinking about the image of vinegar and soda as mentioned in verse 20, we can better understand what King Solomon was telling us. If someone is very sad with a heavy heart, then singing to them – or being merry around them – can actually cause the *opposite* effect: an unsettling or eruptive effect. The person with the heavy heart thinks her friends have no concern for her, and they don't understand how she is feeling. Laughing and showing no sympathy around those who are sad is like taking the peaceful, bitter solution of vinegar and adding baking soda to it. It actually creates an emotionally turbulent condition, making the person sadder because we're not empathizing with them. It seems like we do not care about them.

Can you see the great wisdom in these verses of Proverbs? We can learn from the beautiful similes and visual imagery to demonstrate self-control, bless and encourage those around us, gently speak truth, show kindness, and behave considerately to others.

Day 1:
What is God saying to me?

Think about how your words and actions can affect others. Do you consider your words before you speak? It is so important to think before we open our mouths, particularly when we are talking to someone who is hurting. Are our words and actions showing kindness or are they inconsiderate?

What will I say to God?

This is a great opportunity to thank God for His Word and wisdom in helping us to live and build relationships with those around us. Ask Him to show you ways to love others well. Are you feeling prompted about a relationship you have where there's tension? Have you spoken quickly or harshly? If so, ask God for forgiveness, and then go to the person you're thinking of and ask for their forgiveness.

Reread the lesson's passage and dive deeper.

The verses in this lesson have to do with relationships. God created us as relational people. Yet it can be hard to support friends during times of sorrow, particularly if we haven't experienced what they are going through. Here are some helpful principles to help us be intentional and faithful when a friend is going through a season of hurt.

James 1:19 – *Be quick to listen and slow to speak*. Sometimes it is better to be present and listen instead of saying anything. And when we do speak, it just might be enough to acknowledge that our friend is hurting. Just remember, even though we have a heart to "make it all better" right away, sometimes long-term hurts can't be fixed that way. We can trust together that God will work in His perfect timing.

Galatians 6:2 – *Bear one another's burdens, and so fulfill the law of Christ*. As I mentioned when I shared my story in the previous Dormancy lesson, it was such a blessing to me to receive help from friends and family during that time of hardship. Now, I always like to be on the giving side of things. It was hard for me to receive help. Yet, I remember a friend who wanted to bring a meal one day, and as I tried to stumble my way through not wanting to accept (yet needing the help) she said to me, "Listen. It would bless me to do this. If you don't allow me to bless you, you're preventing me from getting the blessing of doing it." Well, I didn't know what to say, so I just cried and nodded. Let me encourage you to be there for others. It may be awkward, but it will be beautiful!

James 5:16 – *Therefore, confess your sins to one another and pray for one another, that you may be healed. The prayer of a righteous person has great power as it is working*. I know… "read the Bible and pray" is given as the answer to everything. But it is for good reason. Oftentimes those who are hurting have no words to give to God. Pray with them. Let them know you are praying for them. This is the messy part of relationship building, but this is how we love those who are hurting.

We are encouraged to build relationships with others as we build and grow our relationship with Jesus. Verse 11 illustrates how words spoken at the proper time are like golden apples in silver settings. They are precious. Reflect on these ways we can avoid "pouring soda on vinegar."

Old Testament/New Testament Connection

James 2:15-16 says, *If a brother or sister is poorly clothed and lacking in daily food, and one of you says to them, "Go in peace, be warmed and filled," without giving them the things needed for the body, what good is that*? A flippant response to one who is suffering might sound like we mean well, but think of how it might affect the other person. It's so easy to tell someone you will pray for them if they are experiencing trouble. But if we find ourselves just saying those words as a well-meant sentiment without truly intending to pray, are we doing the same thing as the Old Testament verse that pours soda on vinegar? Are we being caustic? Ask God to reveal to you situations where you can be truly compassionate. How can you exhibit kindness and love in a Christ-like way? Is doing this the easy path? And if it's not easy, is it worthwhile?

What is the key point of this lesson for me, and how can I apply it?

Read the following verses that deal with grief and write a few words to remind you how you can be a comfort to others who might be suffering.

John 16:22
Romans 8:18
Psalm 34:18
Matthew 11:28-30
Psalm 147:3
Psalm 73:26

Colossians 4:2-6

² Devote yourselves to prayer, being watchful and thankful.

³ And pray for us, too, that God may open a door for our message, so that we may proclaim the mystery of Christ, for which I am in chains.

⁴ Pray that I may proclaim it clearly, as I should.

⁵ Be wise in the way you act toward outsiders; make the most of every opportunity.

⁶ **Let your conversation be always full of grace, seasoned with salt, so that you may know how to answer everyone.**

1) What is the text saying? Whenever we study a group of verses, it is important to look at their location within a book. You see, the book of Colossians is a letter written to the church in the city of Colossae from the apostle Paul while he was in prison. So this letter has a train of thought, and this passage is a continuation of that. Thus, it is important to remember that this segment in Chapter 4 is on the heels of the rest of a letter. In this lesson's highlighted passage, Paul asks for prayer (v. 3), particularly that he may clearly proclaim the good news of the gospel (v. 4) to those around him.

Next, he turns the appeal towards the people of Colossae (and really to us today!), reminding them that they should be aware of how they conduct themselves around others, making the time worthwhile (v. 5). Finally, verse 6 encourages us all to fill our conversations with grace, making our words savory, seasoned, and engaging. That way we can wisely and lovingly speak to those around us. Well, doing this requires wisdom, because it's important to know how to talk with people who live in a variety of situations and have very different needs. We should always be ready to respond to those around us so they can see the hope we have in Jesus. Believe it or not, everyone has an instinctive need to know the God who made them. If they are not Christians, they will often feel like something is missing from their lives, and they search for it in the world as they seek fulfillment. But they will not find it in the world.

Fulfillment is found in the gospel; God saves sinners. Let's share that message by making our conversation "seasoned with salt," always ready to give an answer to those who ask – an answer that is filled with truth and satisfies those who are listening (1 Pet. 3:15).

2) What is the nature-truth behind the verses? Looking at the highlighted verse 6, we can focus on what it means to season our conversation with salt. The term "salt" basically refers to a charged metal and nonmetal compound. Table salt, for example, is a simple molecule made of an atom of sodium and an atom of chlorine. Separately, these two elements are dangerous. But when combined, they safely provide critical minerals necessary in our diet. So what does salt do?

First, salt is an enhancer. Think about when you bake cookies. The recipe will always include a small amount of salt. Even though salt isn't sweet, it is necessary for a perfectly delicious cookie. That's because when added in the proper proportion, salt amplifies the flavor of what it is mixed into. So it actually *enhances* the cookie's sweetness. It improves and deepens the flavor of food. If you made a divided cookie recipe where half the batter had no salt and then compared the two batches, the salted batch would taste better. Likewise, we should season our words with the saltiness of the truth – gracious speech – as Paul says. You see, when we speak words filled with grace, we build up and encourage those around us. Speaking words of truth and hope creates an explosion of deliciousness! The words draw people to you and invite them to listen.

Next, salt preserves. Before the days of refrigeration, people would store meats and other foods by salting them. Salt dries out food by removing its water, which makes it difficult for bacteria to grow. Thus, salted food lasts longer. When our *words* are salted, they are lasting. They endure and are not fluffy or empty. People remember what you say when your words are sprinkled with the truth and encouragement of God's Word.

Finally, salt is healing. Salt particles have been shown to kill pathogenic microorganisms by dehydrating their cells. Salt has also been shown to reduce inflammation and remove mucus from airways so people can more easily breathe. This can help with allergies and other respiratory illnesses. Natural salts in our diet provide important minerals like potassium, calcium, and magnesium which benefit the nervous system and provide a healthy calcium balance in the body. Likewise, words seasoned with salt heal. They encourage growth. They are filled with nutrients for our soul. When you speak grace-filled words to others, they will be drawn to our Creator for healing (Proverbs 16:24).

So when you season your conversation with salt, you are adding words of truth, hope, and grace which will make your speech attractive, lasting, and healing!

What is God saying to me?

This lesson is a great continuation of the previous one on chemical reactions. Our words definitely have power and can build up or tear down those around us. Do your words draw in others or do they push them away? Reflect on how you can speak with gracious, salted words. Often when we are quick to speak, we tend to forget to speak with wisdom. Ask God to help you carefully craft your words to those around you. Think of those you can encourage today and purpose to do it!

Day 2:
What will I say to God?

James 1:19 says, *Know this, my beloved brothers: let every person be quick to hear, slow to speak, slow to anger*. We should slowly and carefully craft our words, filling them with grace. Remember, grace-filled words have power; they can be attractive, enduring… and delicious!

I am a people-pleaser. I have a hard time saying or doing things that might upset others. But that can be a big problem. As a child, I regularly struggled between going along with the crowd versus standing up for what was right. Thankfully, God brought into my life many people who helped me see the problem with that, particularly in situations when I had to make a decision to follow God's ways instead of man's ways.

A friend of mine who also struggled with this (I was not alone!) shared with me some great insights. She called people-pleasing what it really was: the fear of man. Prov. 29:25 says, *The fear of man lays a snare, but whoever trusts in the Lord is safe*. She shared that she was afraid of what people would think. She wanted them to like her, so she really didn't want to discuss difficult things. Indeed, God's truth can be a stumbling block to many. It can be offensive. But from our conversations, I realized that His truth was offensive in the same way that a life saver is offensive to a drowning person. It certainly disrupts what is going on – but in a good way! My friend shared with me how she re-framed her thoughts by first confessing to the Lord that her people-pleasing was due to a fear of man, not a fear of God. Then she asked herself what it was she was really afraid of. If she was speaking truth, then any rejection would be a rejection of God, not her. Like the Proverb above states, her safety was in trusting God not trusting people.

That blew my mind. Now, I still struggle with people-pleasing, fear-of-man tendencies, but I have learned to slowly and carefully think about my words and then boldly speak.

I encourage you to take the time to prepare yourself by filling your mind and heart with truth so you'll be ready to share it. Ask God to show you people who need encouragement, particularly the encouragement of the gospel. Ask for boldness. Finally, ask for insight as you speak to others. Let your words be as sweet as juicy peaches in summer and as refreshing as crisp apples in fall!

Day 3:
Reread the lesson's passage and dive deeper.

In the highlighted verse, we are instructed to season our words with salt so we know how to answer everyone. What does this say about preparation? If we should be ready with an answer, we must be in God's Word regularly. This way, we are prepared to share it with others. Read 1 Peter 3:15 and meditate on it. Write this verse out in your own words below. Work on memorizing this verse.

Old Testament/New Testament Connection

Read the following Old Testament verses and write whether they speak of salt being attractive (tasty), enduring, or healing.

Numbers 18:19 *All the holy contributions that the people of Israel present to the Lord I give to you, and to your sons and daughters with you, as a perpetual due. It is a covenant of salt forever before the Lord for you and for your offspring with you.* (HINT: think of what a covenant is.)

Job 6:6 *Can that which is tasteless be eaten without salt, or is there any taste in the juice of the mallow?*

2 Kings 2:20-22 He said, *"Bring me a new bowl, and put salt in it."* So they brought it to Him. Then He went to the spring of water and threw salt in it and said, *"Thus says the Lord, I have healed this water; from now on neither death nor miscarriage shall come from it."* So the water has been healed to this day, according to the word that Elisha spoke.

What is the key point of this lesson for me, and how can I apply it?

Think of salt's tastiness and attractiveness. Do you know someone who always seems to say things that make you feel comforted or encouraged? What characteristics do they have that make them so attractive to talk to? How can you emulate that with your own words to others? Now, think of salt's enduring action. Do you want the words you speak to others to endure? How can you build up instead of criticize? Finally, think of salt's healing qualities. Complaining and venting to others will actually injure their hearts because they take on those negative sentiments and feel worse. So how can you avoid complaining and speak healing words instead? Are you around people who regularly complain? What about on social media? Think of the tone of the words coming from you and from people around you. How can you salt your words with Truth?

Week 10:

Joy Verses Happiness - Laughter
Read Proverbs 17:16-28

Proverbs 17:16-28

¹⁶ Why should a fool have money in his hand to buy wisdom when he has no sense?

¹⁷ A friend loves at all times, and a brother is born for adversity.

¹⁸ One who lacks sense gives a pledge and puts up security in the presence of his neighbor.

¹⁹ Whoever loves transgression loves strife; he who makes his door high seeks destruction.

²⁰ A man of crooked heart does not discover good, and one with a dishonest tongue falls into calamity.

²¹ He who sires a fool gets himself sorrow, and the father of a fool has no joy.

²² **A joyful heart is good medicine, but a crushed spirit dries up the bones.**

²³ The wicked accepts a bribe in secret to pervert the ways of justice.

²⁴ The discerning sets his face toward wisdom, but the eyes of a fool are on the ends of the earth.

²⁵ A foolish son is a grief to his father and bitterness to her who bore him.

²⁶ To impose a fine on a righteous man is not good, nor to strike the noble for their uprightness.

²⁷ Whoever restrains his words has knowledge, and he who has a cool spirit is a man of understanding.

²⁸ Even a fool who keeps silent is considered wise; when he closes his lips, he is deemed intelligent.

1) What is the text saying? The verses throughout this chapter of Proverbs compare the behavior between those who are upright and those who are foolish. The passage above focuses more on examples of foolish behavior and its consequences. A fool does not appreciate wisdom (v. 16). It is foolish to take responsibility for another person's debt (v. 18), to look for ways to sin (v. 19), to lie (v. 20), to take bribes (v. 23), and to speak without thinking (v. 28). Interspersed among those verses are some descriptions of wise behavior. A friend loves at all times (v. 17), the discerning embraces wisdom (v. 24), and one who restrains words shows knowledge (v. 27).

Now, hidden in the middle of all this is an interesting comparison. A joyful heart is good medicine, but the opposite – a crushed spirit – dries up the bones (v. 22). A joyful heart and a crushed spirit are presented as opposite behaviors. The first one is good medicine, while the second dries up the bones. Now, it's important for us to understand the difference between joyfulness and happiness. They are not the same thing. Happiness is a feeling that is based on what is happening around us at a specific moment. It is a natural reaction to something good. But joy is supernatural. It sustains our souls during times of heartache and sorrow. Joyfulness comes not from something great but from Someone great. It comes from our hope in the finished work of Christ who is faithful to give us grace and peace no matter what happens around us. That is our exciting hope which overflows in peace-filled joy! Romans 15:13 says, *May the God of hope fill you with all joy and peace in believing, so that by the power of the Holy Spirit you may abound in hope.* That is contagious to others and encourages them. It is good medicine

2) What is the nature-truth behind the verses? Is a joyful heart helpful to our health? Is it *really* good medicine? Well, this is yet another area showing how God's Word gives us truth! Many recent scientific studies have affirmed that hearty laughter makes you feel better and improves your quality of life. In 2016, a study showed that people who laugh more often experience better emotional and social relationships. Laughter benefits their mental health and their immune system[3]. When you laugh, your body produces less cortisol and epinephrine, which are stress hormones, affecting how your body works. Your body produces these stress chemicals when you are experiencing pressures such as fear or anxiety. Cortisol is the body's alarm system working with the brain to affect your mood. Epinephrine causes an increased heartbeat and blood pressure. Well, laughter reduces these stress hormones. Happiness might make laughter occur for a moment, but joy creates a peace and calmness inside that extends throughout our days. So we feel less stress and internal heart-felt laughter for the long term.

Additionally, if you are feeling sad for long periods of time, neurotransmitter chemicals in your brain become reduced. Neurotransmitters are responsible for sending messages from brain cell to brain cell. So when you are feeling sad or depressed, your brain circuitry does not work well. However, when you laugh and experience joy, these chemicals increase, and brain activity improves.

The biological effects of hearty laughter, then, are stress reduction and mood improvement which benefit your body's health. Yet this is not new information. Proverbs 17:22 says, *A joyful heart is good medicine, but a crushed spirit [sadness] dries up the bones,* and Proverbs 15:13 says, *A glad heart makes a cheerful face, but by sorrow of heart the spirit is crushed.*

Thus, as you go through your day, remember the blessings the Lord has given you: your family, friends, fresh air, food, shelter, and most importantly, His Son, Jesus. Without

---

[3]Yim, J. (2016). Therapeutic benefits of laughter in mental health: A theoretical review. *Tohoku Journal of Experimental Medicine*, 239(3), 243-249. Retrieved from https://www.jstage.jst.go.jp/browse/tjem/-char/en

deserving it at all, God places on us the perfect righteousness and holiness of Jesus, meaning we are seen by God as spotless and perfect…as if we have never sinned. And here is the greater joy: because of this we are in right relationship with God! We don't consider Jesus as a ticket to get into heaven. Rather (and definitely more fulfilling!), because of the finished work of Jesus, we have a place before the throne of God. We can come to Him in worship and praise. We can bring our sorrows and receive love. What a joy! No matter how difficult life gets, nothing can take away our position with Him. Nothing! We can sing with joy during our struggles because we know that we have hope in our Savior and relationship with the Father, Son, and Holy Spirit. And that is good medicine!

Day 1:
What is God saying to me?

Many of us struggle with hardships in life. Even imagined anxiety during difficult world events can cause us to worry. Yet those are real felt emotions, and during those times we risk wallowing in those fears and doubts, actually intensifying the sadness. But God gives us His Word for our encouragement. That is His wisdom for me and for you; it can help us re-frame our struggles in light of His truth. You can trust that as a believer, no matter what the world throws at you, you are dearly loved by your Savior. Our sufferings in this world are temporary. That should bring us joy amidst any sadness. That can allow us to joyfully and heartily laugh. Write your thoughts about this below.

What will I say to God?

Here is where the rubber meets the road. Here is where you can share your deep hurts and anxieties with God, knowing He is the author of your faith. He is your Father who loves you unconditionally. And, believe it or not, He knows your hurts. Read Phil. 4:7 and ask Him for *the peace that surpasses all understanding.*

Day 3:

Reread the lesson's passage and dive deeper.

There is a great difference between joy and happiness. Our key verse doesn't say "A happy heart is good medicine," rather it says "A joyful heart is good medicine." Consider the difference between these words. Look up the word, happy, in the dictionary. Then look up the word, joy. How are they different? Happiness is related to a temporary mood. It is often connected with what is going on around us at specific moments. But joy is more enduring. It is connected more deeply within our hearts. Thus, we can be joyful even as we cry.

When my oldest son got married, I was so happy for him, but I was sad that a chapter of our lives was over. We no longer had all of our children in our household. We *were* expanding our family by adding an amazing daughter-in-law, but there was a sadness that I felt, too. That complicated feeling was joy. I joyfully celebrated this new chapter, even though there was a thread of sadness. Joy is more intentional. Joy has to do with our perspective rather than our feeling. We have to purpose to have joy in this life! And that benefits us in many ways, including our health! What are some ways you can be intentional about framing your experiences with joy?

Day 4:
Old Testament/New Testament Connection

James 1:2-3 says, *Count it all joy, my brothers, when you meet trials of various kinds, for you know that the testing of your faith produces steadfastness.* These verses refer to joy in situations that are definitely not happy ones. Do a word search on "joy" in the Bible. Spend time reflecting on how that is different from happiness. Focus on the joy that we have due to the finished work of Jesus that is our salvation. We can be joyful during our struggles when we have hope in our Savior! Write your thoughts below.

What is the key point of this lesson for me, and how can I apply it?

It's easy to mechanically understand the difference between joy and happiness. But it is much more difficult to walk in joy during trials, isn't it? Are you currently going through a challenging time? Write some of the verses from this lesson on note cards. Place them in specific spots in your home – places where you will see them as you go about your day (the laundry area, above the kitchen sink, next to your bathroom mirror, etc.). These will be sweet reminders of the joy you have with your Savior. He will never leave or abandon you. Write out the words to Deut. 31:8 below.

Week 11:

Selflessness - The Dead Sea
Read Ezekiel 47:6-12

⁶ And He said to me, "Son of man, have you seen this?" Then He led me back to the bank of the river.

⁷ As I went back, I saw on the bank of the river very many trees on one side and on the other.

⁸ **And He said to me, "This water flows toward the eastern region and goes down into the Arabah, and enters the sea; when the water flows into the sea, the water will become fresh.**

⁹ And wherever the river goes, every living creature that swarms will live, and there will be very many fish. For this water goes there, that the waters of the sea may become fresh; so everything will live where the river goes.

¹⁰ Fishermen will stand beside the sea. From Engedi to Eneglaim it will be a place for the spreading of nets. Its fish will be of very many kinds, like the fish of the Great Sea.

¹¹ But its swamps and marshes will not become fresh; they are to be left for salt.

¹² And on the banks, on both sides of the river, there will grow all kinds of trees for food. Their leaves will not wither, nor their fruit fail, but they will bear fresh fruit every month, because the water for them flows from the sanctuary. Their fruit will be for food, and their leaves for healing.

1) What is the text saying? Ezekiel was a prophet who wrote to the people of Judah when they were held captive in Babylon. He tells of visions, prophecies, and signs to help declare and illustrate the message of God to His people. In chapter 47, Ezekiel describes what the Final Kingdom will be like which will include amazing physical changes on Earth. One of those changes will involve the Dead Sea, located just east of modern-day Israel. Its modern name comes from being so salty that most organisms cannot live in it. With the exception of a few types of bacteria and microscopic fungi, organisms such as fish and aquatic plants die in this harsh environment. In fact, the Dead Sea is over nine times saltier than the ocean! Verses 6-12 give an account of a vision Ezekiel had from God where he goes to the bank of the river which flows *down into the Arabah* (v.8). Arabah is the Arabic word for an area just south of the Dead Sea basin. Water flows north from there to the Dead Sea.

Ezekiel explains how this barren area will be transformed within the New Earth. A place where nearly nothing can live will be remade into a place containing *every living creature that swarms* (v.9). It will be so plentiful that fishermen will come from all around to fish there (v.10). Barren, salty areas will give way to lush shores where *all kinds of trees* will produce food each month (v.12). For the Israelites who were held in captivity and whose capital city of Jerusalem was destroyed (Ez. 33), this was a great promise for them. They were encouraged that God had a plan in place for His people. And that plan involved something *even greater* than they had seen *before* their captivity.

2) What is the nature-truth behind the verses? The Dead Sea is an interesting place. Sometimes called the Salt Sea, it is a hypersaline lake on the border between modern-day Israel and Jordan in the Middle East. Its surface is over 1,300 feet below sea level – the lowest terrestrial point on Earth!

Now, *hypersaline* is just a fancy word for extra, extra salty. The Dead Sea contains high concentrations of sodium chloride (table salt) and other mineral salts, making it much saltier than the ocean. Why is the Dead Sea so salty? Well, because it has such low elevation, all the rivers and streams in the area flow down into it. As river and runoff water flows over the land, it picks up salts and other minerals from the ground, carrying them into the Dead Sea. However, there are no rivers that drain *out*! Because it has no outward river flow, any salts that make their way into this body of water, then, are stuck there. In fact, the only way water is removed from the Dead Sea is through evaporation. The desert heat causes lots of water to evaporate, but as it becomes vapor, water will not take the dissolved materials with it. Thus, the Dead Sea gets saltier and saltier each year. So we could say that the Dead Sea continually receives but never gives anything away. It is hoarding its salts. Hoarding creates a dead environment inside.

Do we do that? Are we always receiving but never giving? If so, we are creating a dead environment around us. There is no encouragement to others; there is no refreshment. We can become like the Dead Sea – filled up, but unable to support true life. God calls us to be less self-centered and more others-centered. Only by giving can we be truly fulfilled and have life-giving joy!

What is God saying to me?

Think about this in regards to your relationship with your family and friends. Are you constantly taking? Are you hoarding? Do you have any "river outflow?" Yes, it is important that we get inspiration and encouragement *from* others. But when it comes to *pouring out to* others, we must be intentional, because it doesn't come as easily. What are ways you can intentionally encourage and support those around you?

What will I say to God?

It is easy to look at others with a critical eye. We see our kids' disobedience, our spouse's lack of helping us, our friends' disconnectedness. We are quick to complain or critique. We are more aware of our needs than others' needs. Ask God to mature you as a giver and not just a taker. Ask God to show you ways to bless others in your life, and do it without expectations. Write any ideas down below.

Day 3:

Reread the lesson's passage and dive deeper.

Selflessness is a challenging thing to do. We're born with a love of self. I was surprised to learn that about my children. They were born like little angels in my arms – at least according to my new-mother eyes. But then, something happened. They began to show the same selfish nature I struggle with regularly. In fact, I quickly discovered that some of the first words small children learn are the words "No" and "Mine!" This struggle between selflessness and selfishness is tough. According to theologian J.C. Ryle, selfishness "ruined the rich man's soul, and cleaves to us all by nature" just like our skin is stuck to our bodies.[4] Yet selfishness can be dealt with in only one way.

The motivation to adjust our selfishness to selflessness cannot come from a fear of spending eternity in hell or a hope we have of being in heaven. And we shouldn't think of that change as an obligation – like something we have to pull ourselves out of the mire to accomplish – because that won't motivate us, either. The only way to overcome this struggle is to live in the redemption of Christ and His love for us. It is not about us. In relationship with the God of the universe, we require nothing more. We can fully give to others just like our Savior fully gave for us.

The highlighted verse in Ezekiel refers to the Dead Sea transforming from lifeless to life-giving as our fallen Earth will one day be transformed into the New Earth. Just like the change in us, these changes can only come about from the work of our Lord. Reflect on these ideas, particularly in light of Philippians 2:12-13: *Therefore, my beloved, as you have always obeyed, so now, not only as in my presence but much more in my absence, work out your own salvation with fear and trembling, for it is God who works in you, both to will and to work for His good pleasure.*

[4]Ryle, J.C. (1977). *Practical religion.* Baker Book House.

Old Testament/New Testament Connection

The New Testament has much to say about serving others. 1Thess. 5:11 says, *Therefore encourage one another and build one another up, just as you are doing.*

Luke 6:38 says, *Give, and it will be given to you. Good measure, pressed down, shaken together, running over, will be put into your lap. For with the measure you use it will be measured back to you.*

God's Word is consistent throughout the entire Bible. How do these verses relate to the key passage? What does that mean to you?

What is the key point of this lesson for me, and how can I apply it?

Have you ever given a gift to someone that was a complete surprise to them? Perhaps it was a special item you just knew they would enjoy. Remember how it felt to watch them open the present? The joy of giving to others and sharing in their excitement is such a blessing.

Well, the analogy of the Dead Sea and selfishness is a pretty powerful one. Continually taking creates a lifeless environment. We don't ever want to be like that, but it is often difficult to remember that truth. Isn't it amazing how God uses His creation as pictures for us? The verses in Ezekiel are written for us as relevant instruction, applicable today. Ask God for regular reminders to be a giver and an encourager. You will discover that as you pour out to others, more and more will be poured in to you. As our Lord Jesus said, "*It is more blessed to give than to receive*" (Acts 20:35).

What is one way you can bless another person in your life today?

Week 12:
Restlessness - Migration
Read Jeremiah 8:4-7

Jeremiah 8:4-7

⁴ "You shall say to them, Thus says the Lord: When men fall, do they not rise again? If one turns away, does he not return?

⁵ Why then has this people turned away in perpetual backsliding? They hold fast to deceit; they refuse to return.

⁶ I have paid attention and listened, but they have not spoken rightly; no man relents of his evil, saying, 'What have I done?' Everyone turns to his own course, like a horse plunging headlong into battle.

⁷ **Even the stork in the heavens knows her times, and the turtledove, swallow, and crane keep the time of their coming, but my people know not the rules of the Lord."**

1) What is the text saying? Jeremiah was a priest and a prophet to his people in Judah. He was given the hard job of having to tell them to repent and obey God or they would face the judgment of an invading nation (the Babylonians). You see, during Jeremiah's day, the people in Judah worshiped idols and greatly sinned against God. In the passage above, Jeremiah is instructed by God to give the people a message (*You shall say to them…*). His message first begins by explaining how men have a natural instinct to get up when they fall down. In the same way, those who turn away from God have a fundamental need to return to Him (v.4). That desire comes from God revealing Himself to His people both in their hearts and in His writings. But the people of Judah were not behaving that way. Instead, they had turned away from God and were not returning to Him. To further explain this wrong behavior, Jeremiah shares how God-given instincts work even in the animals. Birds such as the stork, turtledove, swallow, and crane have a natural instinct to return to a location from one season to another. Called migration, these animals follow the impulses God has given to them to travel back and forth, returning to their homes each year. However, according to Jeremiah's words, with all of the things that happened to God's people, they never considered the difficulties they were experiencing were a result of their turning away from God without returning. They did not realize they were sinning and had to turn back to God for forgiveness.

2) What is the nature-truth behind the verses? Verse 7 is the highlighted verse in this passage, and it highlights how birds such as storks, turtledoves, swallows, and cranes have the natural instinct to identify the seasons around them and make changes in order to survive. When Jeremiah explains how these birds *keep the time of their coming*, he refers to the migration of these animals as the seasons change. The birds do what is required of them during each season. Yet God's people did not do what God required of them.

Stork migration, for example, is an interesting phenomenon. These birds live on every continent in the world, except Antarctica. Some have wing spans extending over 8 feet long! White storks may have been the birds Jeremiah was writing about. These amazing birds live in northern and central Europe in the summer and migrate to the warmer environments of Sub-Saharan Africa for the winter. This perilous journey can require them to travel for almost 50 days! But the journey is an important one, because they cannot survive the cold northern winters during which food is scarce. Similarly, they will not survive the harsh, hot summers in Africa either, so they must return to their northern homes each spring. If they did not follow their natural instinct to migrate, they would not survive. When they follow their instinctive need to travel south at the beginning of autumn, these birds effortlessly glide for miles at a time, soaring on air updrafts and following thermal air patterns. Interestingly, they cannot travel over the open water of the Mediterranean Sea because large expanses of water do not create the proper air currents for them. That means they will move to the Bosphorus in the East or the Strait of Gibraltar in the West. The Bosphorus pathway is the likely route Jeremiah spoke of as the storks moved across the Middle East on their way to Africa. These pathways funnel large numbers of birds together so thousands can be seen in the sky at one time, sometimes blocking the sun. That must have been a sight people would not have forgotten. So when Jeremiah spoke of migration as a survival instinct, the people would have vividly understood this God-given behavior.

In fact, the more science reveals about how birds migrate, the better we can see how this instinctive, life-giving action is necessary for them. Although not completely understood, we do believe that birds combine many senses as they fly. Compass information from the sun, stars, and even the Earth's magnetic field are combined with visual landmarks and even smells to find their way. In fact, first-year birds of some species are able to make their first migration on their own without help from others. Somehow, they make it to their second home without having seen it before. This desire to migrate is so keen that migratory birds kept in captivity go through a period of restlessness every spring and autumn, fluttering toward one side of their cage regularly. This is called "migratory restlessness." They have an instinctive desire to return to their home.

In the same way, responding to God's prompts for us to return to Him when we sin is necessary to live and enjoy Him forever.

What is God saying to me?

Have you ever felt "migratory restlessness" toward God? God's Word tells us He has given each of us an inner desire for Him. He wants to have relationship with us. Will you be like the stork and listen to that restlessness – that desire to turn to Him? Or will you be like the people in Jeremiah's day and forget how He has revealed Himself to you both in your heart and in His Word? Look up some synonyms for "restlessness" and write them below. Whenever you see a flock of birds in flight, use it as an opportunity to be reminded of the spiritual migratory restlessness we have been given to regularly prompt us to turn back to God.

What will I say to God?

What a blessing that God has given us His Word and has put a natural restlessness in our hearts which can only be fulfilled by knowing Him! In fact, this restlessness is a part of a core human need to know the God who created us. In his book, *Confessions*, St. Augustine of Hippo profoundly stated (speaking to God) that "You have made us for Yourself, and our heart is restless until it rests in You."[5] Perhaps you feel that restlessness today. Are there times when you feel further from God? It is an uneasy feeling, isn't it? Yet, it is such a blessing that God has given us an internal reminder. We feel the pull of relationship with our Father in heaven, and we notice when we are missing out. Ask God to help you seek Him more. Listen to that migratory restlessness in your heart, just as the stork listens to the call to migrate in order to survive.

[5]Augustine. *Confessions*, translated by Rex Warner. New York: Mentor, 1963.

Reread the lesson's passage and dive deeper.

Verse 7 in the passage is a great one to memorize. It is a constant reminder to return to the Lord. The world around us can be so distracting and many things can seem to take over our days. The needs of our family, work, even things like car repairs or household projects can often take precedence over time with our Lord, making it easy to drift away.

I often struggled with finding time to spend in the Word. Life was busy as we raised our children, kept the home, worked, did laundry, and more. There were seasons when I had absolutely no extra time in my day for a quiet time. Of course, my expectations of a quiet time were quite grand. I envisioned quiet time as a morning routine in a calm, silent household, with the sun coming up, producing glorious colors in the sky. I would have a cup of hot coffee or tea in my hand, and I would have plenty of time to read, think, pray, and just take in the morning.

Of course, that never happened when our children were young. They always seemed to get up before me, and when they did go to sleep at night I was completely spent! I definitely had migratory restlessness enough to try to get creative. But I had to adjust my expectations. No quiet morning peacefulness. No hot cup of coffee. (My coffee was regularly reheated in the microwave anyway because I was pulled six different ways each morning.) I realized that if I wanted to memorize and meditate on a verse throughout the day, I could write it out on sticky notes or notecards and place them around the house. I knew I'd be doing dishes each day. I would definitely be in the laundry area, too. So as I busied myself throughout the day, I could look up at the verse I posted in several places and review it in my mind.

If you struggle with finding time for memorization, I encourage you to find creative ways that work for you. It is so helpful to have God's Word in your heart! It will definitely calm your migratory restlessness.

Memorize verse 7. Reread it and write it out in your own words below. Then work to learn it during the next several days.

Old Testament/New Testament Connection

Look up the following verses and write how they relate to this lesson's passage.
Luke 15:20
Hebrews 4:16
James 4:8

What is the key point of this lesson for me, and how can I apply it?

Life is busy. It's easy to get distracted from what is important because of the pull of the urgent. But if we realize that the rest of our life will run more smoothly because we have nurtured our relationship with God, then we will make it a priority. This takes strategy. Think of how you can restructure your days to include time with the Lord. If you are having a hard time figuring out how to do that, ask those around you for suggestions. You do not have to reinvent the wheel. Just realize that what works for some people might not work for you. Your life situation is different from everyone else's because you are uniquely created. Your family situation is unique, too, because each household is uniquely created, as well. Ask God to give you insight in this.

What are some ways you can build into your schedule critical, life-giving time with the Lord?